A NOTE TO PARENTS

When your children are ready to "step into reading," giving them the right books—and lots of them—is as crucial as giving them the right food to eat. **Step into Reading Books** present exciting stories and information reinforced with lively, colorful illustrations that make learning to read fun, satisfying, and worthwhile. They are priced so that acquiring an entire library of them is affordable. And they are beginning readers with an important difference—they're written on four levels.

Step 1 Books, with their very large type and extremely simple vocabulary, have been created for the very youngest readers. **Step 2 Books** are both longer and slightly more difficult. **Step 3 Books,** written to mid-second-grade reading levels, are for the child who has acquired even greater reading skills. **Step 4 Books** offer exciting nonfiction for the increasingly proficient reader.

Step into Reading™

DINOSAUR DAYS

by Joyce Milton
illustrated by Richard Roe

A Step 2 Book

Random House 🏠 New York

For my nieces,
Kirsten and Erica
—J.M.

To my parents
—R.R.

Text copyright © 1985 by Joyce Milton. Illustrations copyright © 1985 by Richard Roe. All rights reserved under International and Pan-American Copyright Conventions. Published in the United States by Random House, Inc., New York, and simultaneously in Canada by Random House of Canada Limited, Toronto.

Library of Congress Cataloging in Publication Data:
Milton, Joyce. Dinosaur days. (Step into reading . A Step 2 book) SUMMARY: Brief and simple descriptions of the various kinds of dinosaurs that roamed the earth millions of years ago. 1. Dinosaurs—Juvenile literature. [1. Dinosaurs] I. Roe, Richard, ill. II. Title. III. Series: Step into reading book. Step 2 book. QE862.D5M55 1985 567.9 1 84-17861 ISBN: 0-394-87023-9 (pbk.); 0-394-97023-3 (lib. bdg.)

Manufactured in the United States of America   11 12 12 13

STEP INTO READING is a trademark of Random House, Inc.

There are no dinosaurs today.

Not even one.

But sometimes

people find dinosaur bones.

The bones are like
parts of a puzzle.
When they are put together,
you can see
what a dinosaur looked like.

The word <u>dinosaur</u> looks hard.

But it is really easy to say.

Say: DIE-nuh-sor.

<u>Dinosaur</u> means "terrible lizard."

Millions of years ago

the world belonged

to the dinosaurs.

In the days of the dinosaurs

there were no people.

No dogs or cats.

No horses or cows.

What animals were there?

Turtles.

Crocodiles.

Fish.

Dragonflies.

The world was very warm
and very wet.

One of the very first dinosaurs
to live on earth
was named Saltopus.
SAWL-tuh-puss

Saltopus lived near a river.

The river was full

of giant crocodiles.

When these giants got hungry,

they came after Saltopus.

SNAP! went the giants' jaws.

SNAP! SNAP!

Then Saltopus stood up

on its strong back legs

and ran away as fast as it could.

Saltopus was fast.

It could run and leap.

That is how it got its name.

<u>Saltopus</u> means "leaping foot."

Saltopus was a small dinosaur.

About the size of a chicken.

Dinosaurs came in many sizes.

Some were small like Saltopus.

Some were big.

And some

were very, very big.

One of the biggest
was Brontosaurus.
BRON-tuh-SOR-us

This dinosaur was

as tall as a house,

longer than two buses,

and as heavy

as five elephants!

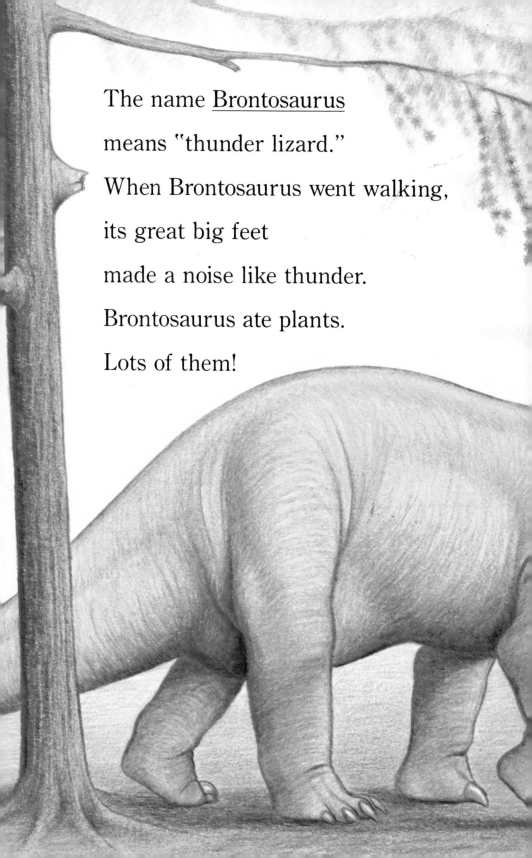

The name <u>Brontosaurus</u>
means "thunder lizard."
When Brontosaurus went walking,
its great big feet
made a noise like thunder.
Brontosaurus ate plants.
Lots of them!

Other dinosaurs

hunted for meat to eat.

One meat eater

was named Allosaurus.

AL-uh-SOR-us

When a hunter dinosaur

came around,

what did Brontosaurus do?

One thing it could do was hide.

Where? Under water!

This dinosaur was fat and slow.

It could not run and hide.

But it did not need to!

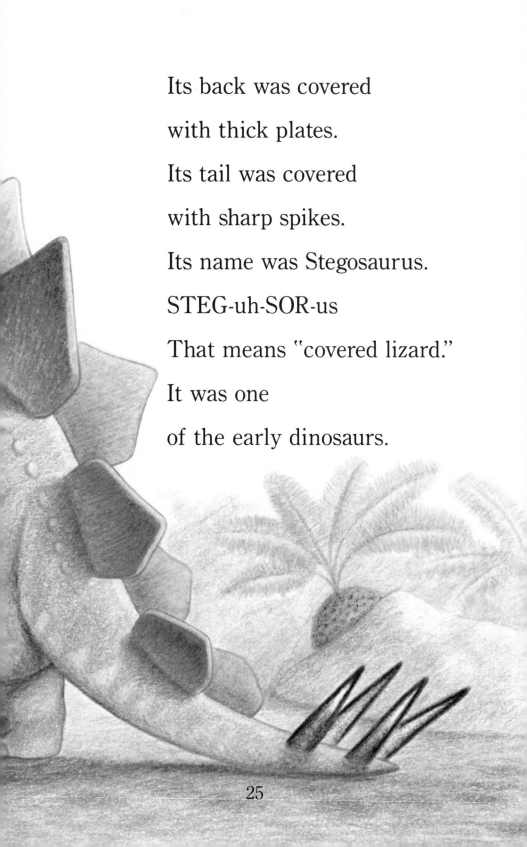

Its back was covered
with thick plates.
Its tail was covered
with sharp spikes.
Its name was Stegosaurus.
STEG-uh-SOR-us
That means "covered lizard."
It was one
of the early dinosaurs.

Not all kinds of dinosaurs

lived at the same time.

Early kinds

like Brontosaurus

died out.

And new kinds

took their place.

Some of the newer dinosaurs
looked a little like ducks.
They are called
duck-billed dinosaurs.

This duck-billed dinosaur

is called Anatosaurus.

an-AT-uh-SOR-us

That means "duck lizard."

Anatosaurus had lots of teeth.

Two thousand of them!

It used its teeth

to mash up plants.

What dinosaur

had the biggest teeth of all?

Tyrannosaurus Rex.

tie-RAN-uh-SOR-us REKS

Its teeth were as long as pencils
and very, very sharp.
The word <u>rex</u> means "king."
This dinosaur was the king
of the hunters.
What did it hunt?
Other dinosaurs!

Some dinosaurs

had ways to keep safe

from Tyrannosaurus Rex.

This dinosaur

had hard plates on its back.

The plates were like armor.

When danger was near,

it just sat tight.

The name of this dinosaur

is Ankylosaurus.

an-KIE-luh-SOR-us

Ankylosaurus also had

a strong tail.

It could swing its tail

like a club.

This dinosaur

used its sharp horns

for fighting.

When it came running,

everyone got out of the way!

Its name is Triceratops.

try-SER-uh-tops

That means "three horns on the face."

There are many things

we do not know

about the dinosaurs.

We think most of them

were brown or green.

But we don't know for sure.

Maybe some were brightly colored.

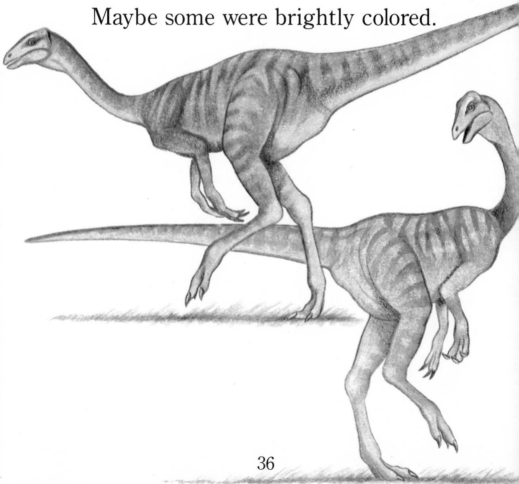

We do know

how dinosaurs were born.

They hatched from eggs,

just like baby birds!

Some dinosaur eggs

were big...

bigger even than a football.

But some were only the size

of a potato.

This dinosaur

is named Protoceratops.

PRO-tuh-SER-uh-tops

The mother made her nest in the sand.

She laid many eggs at one time.

Did she sit on the eggs?

Probably not. She was too heavy.

The eggs might break!

When the babies were born,

they were very small.

Much, much smaller

than their parents.

You could hold

a baby Protoceratops

in your two hands.

In the days of the dinosaurs
strange animals
lived in the sea.
They were real-life sea monsters.
Some of these monsters
looked like dinosaurs.

But they were not dinosaurs.

They were called Plesiosaurs.

PLEE-zee-uh-SORS

They had long necks.

They reached into the water

to catch fish.

Other strange animals
flew in the air.
One of these animals
was Pteranodon.
ter-AN-uh-don
Its body was no bigger
than a turkey's.
But its wings were as wide
as the wings of a small plane.

Pteranodon flew far out to sea.

It rested on the tops of waves.

When it took off,

it soared on the wind

like a glider.

The days of the dinosaurs

lasted a very long time.

Millions and millions of years.

Then a time came

when there were no dinosaurs.

What killed them all?

Maybe the world got too hot.

Maybe the dinosaurs could not find

the right food to eat.

Maybe other animals

ate the dinosaurs' eggs.

Some people even think

the trouble was caused

by a comet

that came too near the earth.

No one knows for sure
what happened.
But in time new animals
took the place
of the dinosaurs.

Dinosaur days

were gone forever.